hc

Working for our Future

Ending Poverty and Hunger

Judith Anderson with Christian Aid

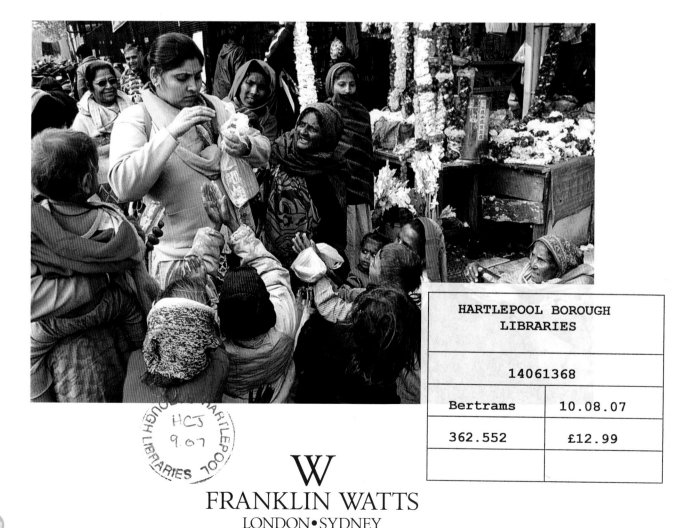

FRANKLIN WATTS
LONDON • SYDNEY

First published in 2007 by
Franklin Watts
338 Euston Road
London NW1 3BH

Franklin Watts Australia
Level 17/207 Kent Street
Sydney NSW 2000
Copyright © Franklin Watts 2007

Editor: Jeremy Smith
Art director: Jonathan Hair
Design: Rita Storey

Produced in association with Christian Aid.

Franklin Watts would like to thank Christian Aid for their help with this title, in particular for allowing permission to use the information concerning Chus Echevarría, Binta Tapile and Servina Marta which is © Christian Aid. We would also like to thank the parents of Shauna Adams for the information and photographs provided.

Picture credits: Adrian Arbib/Christian Aid: 3br, 10l, 13t, 16b, 24b. Alamy: 1, 4b, 6t, 10t, 11b, 13b, 25. Annabel Davis/Christian Aid: 3bc, 6b, 7, 12t, 20-21 all. Eduardo Martino/Christian Aid: 3bl, 8-9 all, 15b, 19b, 23t. istockphoto.com: 27b.

Dewey Classification 362.5

ISBN: 978 0 7496 7344 4

Printed in China

Franklin Watts is a division of Hachette Children's Books.

The Millennium Development Goals

In 2000, government leaders agreed on eight goals to help build a better, fairer world in the 21st century. These goals include getting rid of extreme poverty, fighting child mortality and disease, promoting education, gender equality and maternal health and ensuring sustainable development.

The aim of this series is to look at the problems these goals address, show how they are being tackled at local level and relate them to the experiences of children around the world.

Contents

The Cast

In this book, follow the stories of these four children from around the world, all affected by poverty in different ways.

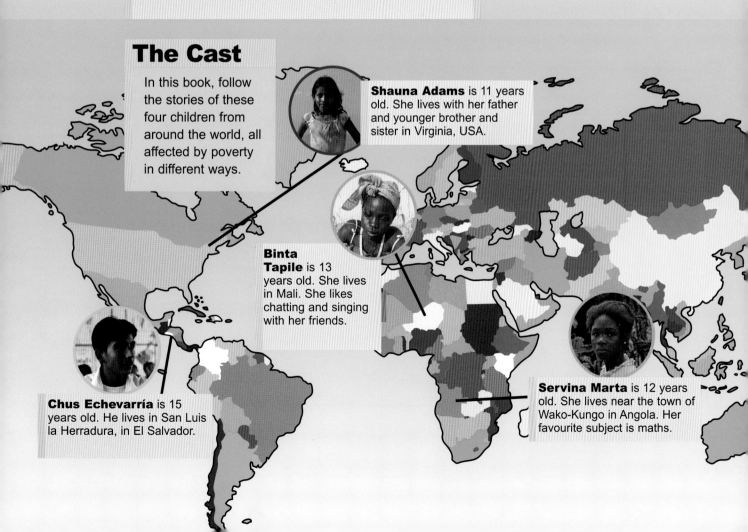

Shauna Adams is 11 years old. She lives with her father and younger brother and sister in Virginia, USA.

Binta Tapile is 13 years old. She lives in Mali. She likes chatting and singing with her friends.

Servina Marta is 12 years old. She lives near the town of Wako-Kungo in Angola. Her favourite subject is maths.

Chus Echevarría is 15 years old. He lives in San Luis la Herradura, in El Salvador.

Living well

We all need food, water and shelter to survive. Fortunately, many of us don't have to worry about these things. We have water in our taps, food on our plates and a comfortable home to return to each night.

This supermarket offers shoppers a selection of food from all over the world.

Food

Food is one of our most basic needs. Eating plenty of different types of food helps us grow strong and stay healthy. It keeps our brains and bodies working and can even prevent some diseases. For most of us, mealtimes are an important part of each day.

‟ We get to choose what we want. My favourite is baked potato with cheese. It fills me up for the afternoon. „

James, aged nine, lives in Scotland. He likes eating school dinners.

Where does it come from?

We either grow our food ourselves or buy it in shops and markets. In more developed countries, there is a huge variety to choose from. This is partly because developed countries can afford to package or freeze food and transport it long distances. They can also afford to import different foods from other countries around the world.

This Indian family are sharing a nutritious meal together. There is plenty of delicious food to eat.

Too much food?

Many wealthier countries actually produce too much food. Much of this good, nutritious produce is wasted when it passes its sell-by-date – the date after which food experts say it is no longer safe to eat. At the end of the day it is simply thrown away.

> 66 More than one quarter of America's food, or about 96 billion pounds (43 billion kg) of food a year, goes to waste - in fields, kitchens, manufacturing plants, markets, schools, and restaurants. 99

A statistic from the US Environmental Agency. Much of the food we throw away is perfectly safe to eat.

? What will you eat and drink today? Where has it come from? How can you find out?

Feeling hungry

What happens when you feel hungry? Do you get tired? Do you find it difficult to concentrate on anything else? We soon feel better if we eat a snack or sit down to a meal. Food is never far away. However, for some people, obtaining food is not so easy.

Binta Tapile from Mali describes how she struggled to find enough to eat last year when crops were destroyed by grasshoppers.

❝ Sometimes I'd sleep without eating. It's very difficult and I don't like it. You spend the night hungry and in the morning it's worse. ❞

▲ A mother and her children beg for food in Jaipur, India.

Not enough to eat

In some parts of the world, people are starving. This means that they will die unless they obtain something to eat. In many more parts of the world, people do manage to buy or grow some food but they are still not getting enough food or the right food to keep them healthy. They face a daily struggle to feed themselves and their families. They are malnourished.

The effects of hunger

Food gives us energy. Without it we feel irritable. Our bodies cannot grow properly and we may feel too weak to study or earn money. We are unable to concentrate. We are also much less able to fight off sickness and disease.

Today, nearly one in seven people worldwide do not get enough food to be healthy and live an active life. This is despite the fact that many people in the developed world have more than enough to eat.

▲ The round bellies of these children are caused by a severe lack of the kinds of food they need for growth and energy.

The effects of starvation are very serious. Binta describes what happened when she went without food for a while.

❝ We had six days with no food at all. I was very skinny, I was sick, my stomach hurt and I had pains all over. I couldn't walk. I felt light-headed. **❞**

❓ Why is a healthy diet particularly important for children like Binta?

Under a dollar a day

What can you buy for one dollar or about 50 pence? A bag of crisps? A carton of juice? It won't stop you from feeling hungry for very long. Yet over one fifth of the world's population survive on less than a dollar each day.

The "poverty trap"

The main reason for hunger is poverty. People do not have enough money to get the food they need. And a hungry person is less able to earn money because they have no time or energy to work or learn new skills. All their strength is taken up with trying to secure the next meal for their families. So they remain poor. This is known as the "poverty trap".

Chus Echevarría lives in El Salvador with his brother and sister and her family. He helps to support his family.

Chus goes to school in the morning and works collecting crabs in the evening.

❝ The work we do to earn our food is not easy. I began working when I was eight. I help my sister's husband catch crabs and carry them for him. **❞**

❝ I keep a dozen of the crabs we catch to feed the family: that's enough for two meals, lunch and supper (the crabs are very small). **❞**

Chus uses the money he earns to buy bread for his family. His sister Domenica prepares the crabs Chus has caught.

Children in poverty

Many children around the world must work in order to buy or grow food for themselves and their families. But children who are herding cattle, fetching water or selling vegetables all day cannot go to school to learn the skills they need to end the poverty trap. Other children must work as well as going to school. School means they have a better chance of ending the poverty trap, but their day is often long and hard.

Chus earns around a dollar a day from the crabs he catches. Once money has been used to pay for food, Chus spends what is left on school books and his school uniform.

 How is Chus's life different from yours?

The world's poor

Billions of people go hungry every day because they cannot afford to buy food. But why don't they have any money? What makes them poor? Poverty is caused by many different things.

▲ A maize crop withers away in the field because of severe drought in Tanzania, Africa.

Drought and war

Drought, or lack of rain, devastates whole regions of the world each year. No rain means crops cannot grow and animals die. Farmers cannot feed their families and have nothing to sell at the market.

War also affects farmers. Crops and animals are stolen, abandoned or destroyed. People may be forced to leave their homes and farms. They lose their livelihoods.

Servina Marta, aged 12, lives with her parents in Angola. When war came, they had to leave their village home and flee to safety. They lost everything. They returned to the village in great poverty.

❝ My mum and dad built a little cabin before they sent for us. There wasn't much food. **❞**

Shauna Adams lives in Virginia, USA. Her father works long hours as a lorry driver but he doesn't earn enough to pay the bills.

" I can't remember the last time I bought anything for myself. "

Jobs and wages

Another reason for poverty is unemployment, when people cannot find work. This may be because they do not have the right skills, or perhaps there aren't enough jobs to go round. Others cannot work because they are ill or disabled.

Many working people are paid very low wages. They may not have the skills needed to find a better job.

Chinese textile manufacturers at work. These women do not earn enough to provide a good quality of living for their families.

Is poverty a problem in your country? Can you think of any reasons for this?

Coping with famine

In some parts of the world, whole regions suffer from severe food shortages, known as famine. Famine is a particular problem in areas of Asia and Africa where lack of rain or heavy flooding means crops die and farmers cannot feed their families. It disrupts people's lives and causes them to move around in constant search of money and food.

Binta's village in Mali has suffered because of a plague of grasshoppers.

❝ We have four fields but we had no harvest at all because there has been no rain and the grasshoppers have eaten all our plants. When I think of grasshoppers, I think of famine. I am afraid I will be hungry again. **❞**

Famine in Africa

Drought is a main reason for famine in Africa. However, it is not the only reason. War has forced many people to abandon their homes and farms. Diseases such as malaria and HIV/AIDS mean that farmers may be too sick to work. Farming methods are often not very efficient and governments may fail to store enough grain and seed for use in an emergency.

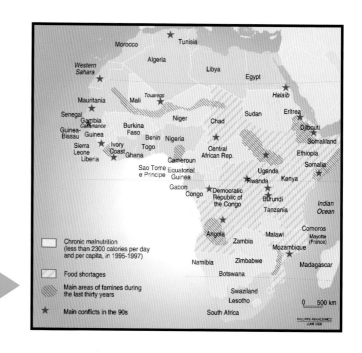

This map of Africa shows the main areas of famine and malnutrition in recent years.

> **"** I had to cut firewood and take it to the city to sell. I had to leave home at about 8 o'clock and I got to Wako-Kungo at about 11 o'clock. I carried the firewood on my head. It was very heavy. **"**

Servina had to travel a long way from her village in order to make money.

Towns and cities

Famine does not just affect farmers. It affects people in towns and cities too. Food prices go up which makes it more difficult for people to eat properly. People travel from the countryside to the city to try to find work but often there are not enough jobs to go round. The cycle of poverty continues.

▼ Poor people beg for money in one of the crowded slum areas in Delhi, India. People flock to the city in search of jobs.

? Binta is afraid that she will be hungry again. Do you think the rest of the world should try to help people like her?

The Millennium Development Goals

Poverty is responsible for much of the suffering in the world today. In the year 2000, the world's leaders met at the United Nations and agreed a set of eight goals that would help to make the world a better, fairer place in the 21st century. These goals were named the Millennium Development Goals. The first goal is to get rid of extreme poverty and hunger.

Some of the world leaders who attended the G8 Summit to tackle world poverty.

The Goals

Each goal has particular targets that need to be achieved by the year 2015 and governments have been asked to develop policies that will ensure these targets are met. The target for the first goal is to halve by 2015 the number of people living in extreme poverty.

THE EIGHT MILLENNIUM DEVELOPMENT GOALS

1 Get rid of extreme poverty and hunger

2 Primary education for all

3 Promote equal chances for girls and women

4 Reduce child mortality

5 Improve the health of mothers

6 Combat HIV/AIDS, malaria and other diseases

7 Ensure environmental sustainability

8 Address the special needs of developing countries, including debt and fair trade

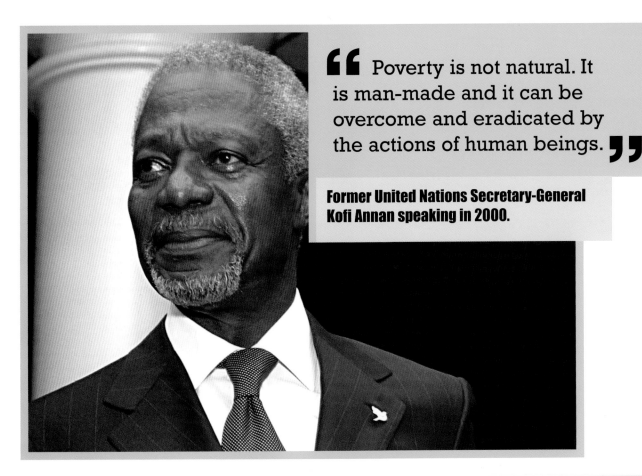

"Poverty is not natural. It is man-made and it can be overcome and eradicated by the actions of human beings."

Former United Nations Secretary-General Kofi Annan speaking in 2000.

A brighter future

Every child has the right to a life free from poverty and hunger. Binta hopes to become a doctor. Chus wants to be an engineer. The Millennium Development Goals are designed to help them achieve their aims.

"I'd like to study to be an engineer because I like drawing and they build homes and useful buildings."

Chus hopes to change his life in the future.

? **Which Millennium Development Goals would help Binta and Chus make a better life for themselves and those around them?**

Emergency aid

Hungry people need food. If they are starving, this food has to be found quickly. There is no time to grow it. It must be brought in from somewhere else. This is known as "emergency aid". Sometimes the government provides it. Sometimes a charity or an aid organization sends it.

Villagers receive emergency aid rations during the war in Iraq.

Access to food

Emergency aid saves millions of lives every year. Once people get food their strength returns and they can begin to farm again, or look for work. Mothers can care for their babies. Children can go back to school. They can start to think about the future.

" They gave us 10 kg of maize and 6 kgs of beans to plant and also some oil, salt and lentils. If ACM hadn't come to help us, we'd be dead. "

Servina's mother remembers being given emergency aid. Here, Servina's younger sister Rosaria pounds maize outside their home.

When people from Servina's village returned to their homes in Angola at the end of the war, crops had been destroyed and they had nothing to eat. An organisation called Associaçáo Cristáde Mocidade (ACM) quickly brought in emergency supplies of food for those most at risk of starvation. They gave porridge with added nutrients to the youngest children, and distributed grain to the worst affected families. They also gave people maize seeds to plant so that crops could be re-established as quickly as possible.

Hunger in the developed world

Hunger and poverty exist in "richer" countries as well as the developing world. Shauna lives in the USA yet her family struggles to make ends meet. They rely on aid from local charities to get by each month.

❝ Often there isn't enough money to last the month, so we rely on charities such as Save the Children. **❞**

Shauna's life is a constant struggle. She has to buy the cheapest food, even though she knows it isn't very healthy.

? **Millions of people rely on emergency aid for their survival. Can you think of any problems this might create?**

Government action

Emergency aid solves the problem of hunger, but it does not solve the problem of poverty. Poverty can only be ended when people no longer depend on emergency aid. They need to be able to grow their own food and earn their own money. For this to happen, a different kind of help is needed.

What governments can do

Governments can agree to change things so that poor people have the freedom, the knowledge and the tools to help themselves in the future. They can support poorer farmers, helping them to use the land in a more efficient way. They can change the rules of international trade so that poorer countries can buy and sell goods for a fairer price. This is called "fair trade". They can make sure that resources are shared in times of drought or famine.

❝ It's really very simple. When people are hungry they die. So spare me your politics and tell me what you need and how you're going to get it to these people. ❞

The FAIRTRADE Mark shows that the producer has been given a fair price and a better deal.

The singer Bob Geldof (shown above left with Jacques Chirac (centre) and Bono) uses the slogan "Make Poverty History" to persuade world leaders to change their policies and reduce the debts of poorer countries.

FAIRTRADE

Guarantees a **better deal** for Third World Producers

Debt

One of the biggest problems for poor countries is debt. They borrow money from more developed countries but they can't afford to pay this money back. Now some governments have agreed to reduce the amount of money owed to them. This means that poorer countries have more money to spend on improving the lives of their own people.

A delegation of African women deliver over 150,000 white band cards to Tony Blair from supporters of the "Make Poverty History" campaign, demanding that the UK does more to ensure better aid, fairer trade and no more debt.

Chus was asked what he would do if he was president for a day.

" I'd send help to all those with no resources. "

? What would you do if you were in charge for the day?

Local solutions

Change at local level is just as important in improving the lives of children like Binta, Servina, Chus and Shauna. All over the world, charities and community support groups are bringing about lasting change through local solutions to specific problems.

Belco Seiba is a brigadier (see below) from Binta's village who trains villagers to prevent grasshopper crop destruction.

" The brigadiers have trained the rest of the community to dig for the egg larvae. For one piece of larvae we are securing 8 – 10 square metres of crops. **"**

A pesticide spray used to protect crops.

A bowl of grasshopper eggs collected by Binta.

New tools and skills

Charities and community support groups give practical help at a local level. This includes providing the right tools and seeds so that people can begin to grow their own food. Teaching people new skills is equally important if they are to farm more efficiently, or find better-paid work.

Helping people help themselves

To fight the grasshoppers in Mali, Binta's village have a team of APH/Christian Aid funded brigadiers (leaders). Volunteers from the community are trained to monitor locust and grasshopper movements, protect crops and undertake crop spraying.

> **❝**If I get a lot of eggs I take them home for my mother, and as soon as we have collected enough we rush off to exchange them for millet.**❞**

Binta and her friends are destroying grasshopper eggs. She helped collect them.

APH also tried to prevent the insects from coming back by encouraging people to find and destroy grasshopper eggs. For every kilogram of eggs that were destroyed, APH handed out 2 kgs of millet as a reward.

Long-term benefits

When a charity or a local support group introduces new skills and resources into a community, the benefits are often long-term. Building a water storage tank, introducing drought-resistant crops or providing information about good health practices mean that people will be able to take care of themselves and cope better with any problems in the future.

? APH have given seeds to the women in Binta's village so that they can grow onions. How will this help Binta and her mother?

People who help

Some of the people who work for aid organisations are volunteers. Others are employed because of their skills as nutritionists, agricultural experts, scientists or managers. All of them want to help improve the lives of those living in poverty.

Different backgrounds

People who work for change come from all sorts of backgrounds, cultures and faiths. Some come from more developed countries and bring specialised skills. Aid organisations also try to employ local people who have a good understanding of the problems in their particular region.

Teaching skills

William Anderson manages a drought recovery programme for Christian Aid in Zimbabwe. He sees it as his duty to pass on the skills that will allow people to help themselves in the future. This kind of action is happening across poor areas in Africa, South America and areas of the developed world where people are not so fortunate.

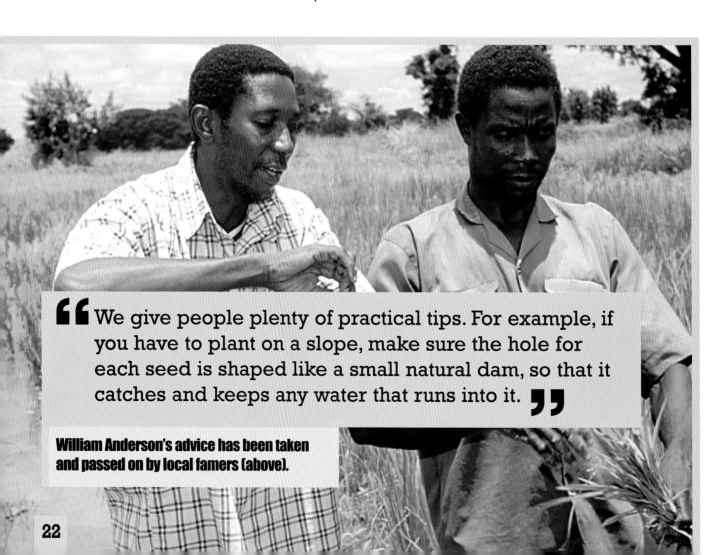

" We give people plenty of practical tips. For example, if you have to plant on a slope, make sure the hole for each seed is shaped like a small natural dam, so that it catches and keeps any water that runs into it. **"**

William Anderson's advice has been taken and passed on by local famers (above).

Aprodehni in action

Gloria Ventura de Rivera was the director of Aprodehni, an organisation that assists people in the area of El Salvador where Chus lives. This is what happened when Hurricane Stan struck the region.

> **" Aprodehni goes into action when there's a red alert. We had to distribute food despite the danger, and children were the priority. "**

When Hurricane Stan struck Chus's village, he worked with Aprodehni to fill sandbags and build up a flood defence system.

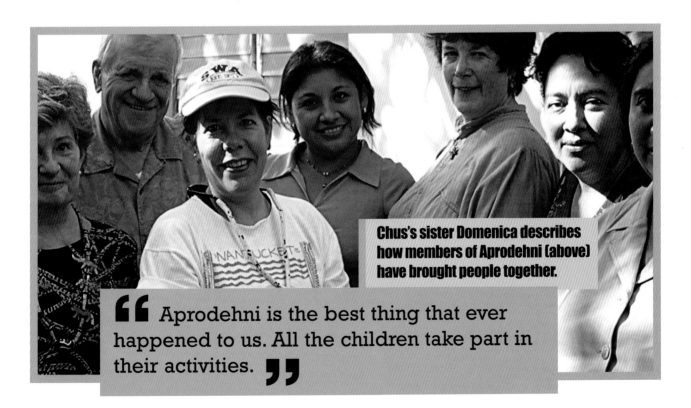

Chus's sister Domenica describes how members of Aprodehni (above) have brought people together.

> **" Aprodehni is the best thing that ever happened to us. All the children take part in their activities. "**

? Have you ever tried to help someone who is having problems? How did it make you feel?

Growing food

Ending hunger is not just about providing food. It is about making sure that people can get it in the future. For millions of people around the world, the only way to do this is to grow it themselves.

Teaching people to grow nutritious crops such as rice (right) and wheat is essential to helping them escape poverty in the long term. ▶

Getting started

When Servina's family returned to their village after the war in Angola, a local organisation called ACM came and gave them food to eat. They also gave them the tools and seeds they needed to grow maize and beans. Some of the crops were attacked by insects the first year, and didn't grow well. However, the following year they had enough maize left to plant a bigger crop.

Servina enjoys the family's improved diet.

❝ We had *funge* (a kind of flour pudding) and beans this morning and we will have funge and pumpkin leaves for lunch. We'll have something for dinner. **❞**

Enough for everyone

Now Servina's family have been given a pair of oxen and a plough. This means that they will be able to cultivate even more land. In the future they hope to be able to grow enough food to sell some of it and return some to ACM so that others can benefit from it. They also hope that ACM will give them some goats, which are good for milk and meat.

❝ We bought 12 oxen to deliver to six families in six different villages. The calves will be given to other families in the village. Other families will also be able to borrow the plough and the oxen. **❞**

Nunes de Oliveira Mario, ACM's project coordinator, explains how the oxen will be used.

❝ I like the oxen. They don't have names yet but I want to call the girl ox Umba. I like Umba best. The other one has horns and I'm a bit scared of him. **❞**

The oxen will help to bring Servina's family out of poverty.

? **Now that Servina has more to eat, what difference will this make to her life?**

Equal opportunities

Poverty affects children in many ways. It affects the food they eat, the homes they live in and limits their access to good healthcare, sport and a proper education. Ultimately a child trapped in poverty does not have the same chances as other children.

" I want to get good grades at school, go to school dances and get into college. **"**

Shauna states her ambitions for the future.

Shauna's story
Shauna Adams lives in Virginia, USA with her father and younger brother and sister. The family isn't starving and Shauna's father has a job but his wages are low. Shauna, who takes care of the other children before and after school, is forced to buy cheap processed food that is bad for their health. Shauna dreams of going to college but worries that she may have to stay at home to provide for the family and look after her father who has a heart condition and who cannot afford health insurance.

Shauna has few places to go where she lives. She spends a lot of time at the local community centre (left).

" The problem around here is that they don't teach you how to dream. **"**

A better life

Some children in Shauna's area are being supported by Upward Bound, an organisation that helps poorer children go to college by offering advice on how to improve their grades and get a scholarship so that they do not have to pay expensive fees. Others can join Step-by-Step, a local organisation that runs youth programmes to build confidence and self-esteem in her area. With the right guidance, children from poorer backgrounds all over the world can be encouraged to raise their expectations and look towards gaining a proper education.

TRiO
U P W A R D   B O U N D

Organisations such as the state-run Upward Bound programme in the United States aim to help children like Shauna realise their dreams.

❝ Kids need to be given the opportunity to create success. Without money or resources, it's difficult for them to build a bigger world for themselves. ❞

Michael Tierney, Director of Step-by-Step, explaining why the poorest children need a helping hand to make a start in life.

? Children like Shauna need support from their peers as well as money. How could you help someone like Shauna?

Action you can take

Everyone can take part in the fight against hunger and poverty. One of the most useful things you can do is to make other people aware of the problem. The more people want change, the more change is likely to happen.

Buy fairly traded goods

Look out for brands of coffee, sugar, tea, chocolate, fruit and other goods that carry the Fairtrade symbol. This means that the farmers or producers in developing countries have been paid a fair price for their goods.

Have a "poverty awareness" assembly

Research the reasons for poverty and hunger in a developing country. Use role play to act out a day in the life of a child living in poverty. Then show how, from small beginnings (a few seeds, a goat, a new water pipe) people can start to help themselves and those around them.

Hold a "hunger lunch"

Ask people to go without their usual snacks and offer a bowl of rice or porridge and water instead. The money saved can be collected and donated to a charity helping children in poverty.

Indian cricketer Sachin Tendulkar promotes the UN's "Stand Up Against Poverty" campaign.

Women collect tea in Nepal for sale around the world under the Fairtrade agreement.

christian aid

We believe in life before death

 The official logo of the charity Christian Aid, who help poor children around the world, whatever their religion.

Support a charity

There are many charities working around the world to help people escape the "poverty trap". Choose one and ask them for a schools' pack, posters and information about the work they do. Then start fundraising!

Donating unwanted clothes and other goods is a great way to help people in the developing world.

Donate clothes, shoes and food

Some charities collect second-hand clothes, shoes and items such as glasses for re-use in developing countries. Others run local "food banks" where you can donate dried or tinned food. Find out what these charities do and then think about setting up a collection point at your school.

? If you could meet Chus, Binta, Servina or Shauna, what would you like to say to them?

Glossary

Charity an organisation that uses money donated by members of the public to help others

Debt money that has been borrowed and must be paid back

Developed world countries with more wealthy economies

Developing world poorer countries with poorer economies

Diet what someone usually eats

Drought prolonged lack of rain

Economy The wealth of a country

Fair trade buying goods at a price that ensures farmers and producers have enough to live on and gives long-term commitments

Famine severe food shortages in a particular area, often because of drought or war

HIV/AIDS a disease that leaves the body unable to fight off illness

Malnourished someone lacking the food necessary for good health and growth

Millennium Development Goals (MDGs) eight goals agreed by world leaders in the year 2000 with the aim of eradicating poverty and promoting the rights of disadvantaged people

Mortality rate the number of deaths in a population

Nutritious healthy food that gives us energy and helps us grow

Poverty lack of money for essential items such as food, shelter, medicines or education

Resources things that assist development such as books, equipment, food, seeds and tools

Starving dying from lack of food

Summit a meeting of world leaders

Sustainability something that is designed for the long term

United Nations an organisation of countries around the world with the aim of promoting peace, development and human rights

Find out more

Useful websites

www.un.org/cyberschoolbus
Go to the Millennium Development Goals for accessible and child-friendly facts about the MDGs. Also useful for information about the work of the United Nations.

www.millenniumcampaign.org/goals_ poverty
The latest news, pictures, facts and statistics as well as information about what you can do to help eradicate hunger and poverty.

www.makepovertyhistory.org
The website of the anti-poverty movement.

www.makepovertyhistory.com/au
Learn about trade justice for developing countries.

Note to parents and teachers:
Every effort has been made by the Publishers to ensure that these websites are suitable for children, that they are of the highest educational value, and that they contain no inappropriate or offensive material. However, because of the nature of the Internet, it is impossible to guarantee that the contents of these sites will not be altered. We strongly advise that Internet access is supervised by a responsible adult.

www.maketradefair.com
Find out about fair trade products, news and campaigns where you live by clicking on the country links.

www.papapaa.org
An interactive site for children aged 9-14 that focuses on the need for fair trade practices in cocoa farming.

Christian Aid websites

Christian Aid contributed three of the real-life stories in this book (the accounts of Chus, Binta and Servina). You can find out more about this organisation by following the links below:

www.christian-aid.org.uk
The main site for the charity Christian Aid, who help disadvantaged children and adults all over the world, regardless of their religion.

www.globalgang.org.uk
Christian Aid's website for kids with games, news and stories from around the world.

Index

Contents

Who was Marc Chagall?

Marc Chagall was one of the most popular and distinctive artists of the 20th century. His colourful, dream-like works offer a unique mixture of fantasy, folklore, myth and memory.

Marc Chagall is a French name, adopted by the artist as a young man. He was born Moyshe Segal on 7 July 1887 into a large, poor Jewish family in Vitebsk, a town in western Russia. His Russian Jewish heritage was central to his life and art.

> *'Were I not a Jew, I would not have become an artist.'*
>
> Marc Chagall

EARLY LIFE

Almost all we know about Chagall's early life comes from his autobiography *My Life*, written in 1922 when he was 34. According to his own account, Chagall's birth was accompanied by great drama, as a large fire broke out nearby, and baby Moyshe was placed in a stone market trough for safety.

Chagall was the oldest of nine children. His family were Hassidic Jews, who observed their religious laws and traditions piously. Every day at dawn his father went to the synagogue, before spending the day working for a herring merchant. His enterprising, energetic mother ran a grocery store, with 'herrings in barrels, sugar heaped like pointed heads, flour, candles…'.

SCHOOL DAYS

Vitebsk was home to one of Russia's largest Jewish communities (see panel). Chagall attended the *cheder*, the traditional Jewish primary school, where he learned Hebrew and Biblical history. Jewish children were banned from attending state schools, but Chagall went on to the local state secondary school, after his mother had bribed the headmaster. Here he learned geometry and Russian, which he began to speak as well as Yiddish (the traditional Jewish language).

DRAWING INSPIRATION

According to Chagall, the only pictures in his home were family photographs. He claimed he had never seen a painting or drawn a picture before 1906, when he saw a fellow pupil drawing. It was a revelation, and he too began to draw. He was determined to become an artist.

The 19-year-old Chagall joined a local art school run by a Jewish artist Yehuda Pen (1854-1937), who painted realistic scenes and portraits. Chagall's obvious talent earned him free tuition. He took a job retouching photographs, but the young artist wanted more from life. In the winter of 1906-7, with 27 roubles in his pocket, he set out for the city of St Petersburg, capital and cultural heart of Russia.

▲ Vitebsk c. 1920. Memories of the town and his early life there remained very important to Chagall and his artistic imagery. He remembered its buildings as 'simple and eternal'.

'At Pen's I was the only one to paint in purple. That seemed so bold that from then onwards I attended the school without paying.'

Marc Chagall

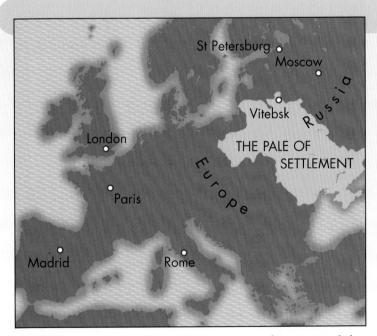

▲ The vast empire of Russia lay to the east of Europe. Vitebsk – close to the Lithuanian border, now in the independent country of Belarus – was in 'the Pale of Settlement' (shown in yellow).

JEWS IN TSARIST RUSSIA

At the time of Chagall's birth, Russia was ruled by the Tsar or emperor. For centuries, Jews had suffered hatred, persecution and segregation. They were only allowed to live in one area known as 'the Pale of Settlement' (see map). Chagall's hometown of Vitebsk was within this area, and about 48,000 of its 65,000 inhabitants were Jews. The town was the stronghold of Hassidic Judaism, a Jewish sect founded in the 1730s by Baal-Shem Tov. His teachings are based on mystical writings known as the *cabbalah*, which preach universal love. Hassidic Jews are noted for their piety – and also for their joyous dancing and chanting. This joy can be seen in Chagall's art, along with many Jewish symbols, but the adult Chagall never really practised his religion.

Poverty in St Petersburg

When the 20-year-old Chagall arrived in St Petersburg, Jews were not allowed to live there without a permit. To get round this, a friend of the family arranged documents stating that Chagall was working for a Vitebsk merchant. Once in the capital, he posed as a servant for a wealthy lawyer in order to be able to stay. Although he mostly managed to keep ahead of the authorities, he once forgot to pay a necessary bribe, and was thrown in prison for several weeks.

▲ A main street in St Petersburg in the late 19th century.

LEARNING HIS TRADE

Chagall enrolled at the School of the Imperial Society for the Protection of the Fine Arts. The school's director, the painter Nicholai Roerich (1874-1947), was very encouraging: he arranged for Chagall to be exempt from military service, and even organised a grant of 15 roubles per month. This was a lifeline for Chagall, who was living in desperate poverty, sharing a room and even a bed!

However, Chagall found the teaching at the art school boring, and the atmosphere cold and depressing. After two years of copying plaster casts, he had had enough – he left the school without even collecting his monthly grant. After studying at a private art school for a couple of months, he enrolled at the Zvantseva School, run by Léon Bakst (1866-1924), now best remembered as a stage designer with the Ballets Russes (Russian Ballet).

▲ Chagall, shortly before he moved to St Petersburg.

TIMELINE ▶

7 July 1887	1906	Winter 1906-7	1907	1908	1909
Moyshe Segal (Marc Chagall) born in Vitebsk.	Chagall enters Yehuda Pen's art school in Vitebsk.	Chagall moves to St Petersburg (without a permit).	Chagall enrols at the School of the Imperial Society for the Protection of the Fine Arts.	Chagall leaves the Imperial Society school. He meets Maxim Vinaver.	Chagall enrols at Zvantseva School. He meets Bella Rosenfeld, his future wife.

▲ Bella Rosenfeld, c. 1910-11. Of his first meeting with Bella, Chagall wrote: 'I have a feeling that this is my wife. Her pale complexion, her eyes. How large, round and black they are! They are my eyes, my soul.'

▶ *The Wedding* (or *Russian Wedding*), 1909. This early painting by Chagall shows a joyful scene from Vitebsk. The young artist used dark colours and painted this traditional scene with a relatively realistic sense of perspective. Chagall's style was to change dramatically when he reached Paris.

> ## 'In France I was born for a second time.'
> Marc Chagall

Chagall later said that it was Bakst who made him aware of 'the breath of Europe' and when Bakst left for Paris, Chagall applied to go with him as his assistant. He was turned down.

BELOVED BELLA

Despite being virtually destitute, Chagall made several visits home from St Petersburg to Vitebsk. During one of these visits, in October 1909, he met Bella Rosenfeld (1895-1944). It was love at first sight for both of them. Bella was to become his beloved wife and muse for more than 30 years.

A FIRST PATRON

In St Petersburg, Chagall had another significant meeting, this time with Maxim Vinaver (1863-1926), an influential member of the Duma, the Russian parliament. Chagall described Vinaver as 'almost like a father'. He sponsored Chagall and bought some of his paintings. Most importantly, he allowed Chagall to travel to Paris – giving him an allowance of 40 roubles a month. In August 1910, Moyshe Segal – by now known as Marc Chagall – arrived in Paris.

A Russian in Paris

▲ *Still Life with a Harp and a Violin*, 1912, Georges Braque.

CUBISM

Cubism was probably the most important art movement of the early 20th century. It was developed by Pablo Picasso (1881-1973) and Georges Braque (1882-1963) in Paris between 1907 and 1914. Creating a new way of representing the world around them, these artists and their followers abandoned the idea of showing objects from a single, fixed viewpoint as Western artists had done for centuries. Instead, they used multiple viewpoints, so that different parts of an object could be seen at the same time. Objects in the real world were broken up into fragments, and put back together on the canvas.

Twenty-three years old and unable to speak French, Chagall was homesick, yet very excited to be in Paris. He attended painting academies, but mainly taught himself by studying Old Masters in the Louvre and contemporary artists at work in the city.

NEW INFLUENCES

Two days after his arrival, Chagall visited the Salon des Indépendants, and saw modern French art for the first time. He encountered the work of the Cubists (see panel) and the Fauves, who included Henri Matisse (1869-1954). The Fauves prompted Chagall to use bright and vibrant colours, while Cubism encouraged him to develop his own unique sense of perspective. In his early masterpiece, *I and the Village*, Chagall blends memories of his Russian home with a fragmented sense of space that reflects his knowledge of Cubism.

'I have brought my subjects from Russia ... Paris has given them light.'

Marc Chagall

▲ La Place de l'Opéra, Paris, 1910. The Opéra stands on the right. Fifty-three years later, Chagall would paint its ceiling (see page 36).

TIMELINE ▶

1910	1911
Supported by a grant from Maxim Vinaver, Chagall moves to Paris in August. He sees modern French art for the first time and attends two private art academies.	Chagall moves into the artists' colony *La Ruche* (the Beehive, see pages 14-15). Here he meets the poets Blaise Cendrars (1887-1961) and Guillaume Apollinaire (1880-1918, see page 16).

I and the Village, 1911

oil on canvas 192.1 x 151.4 cm Museum of Modern Art, New York

A green profile of a man in a peaked cap (probably Chagall) and a white cow stare into each other's eyes, linked by a dotted line. Russian rural scenes are scattered across the canvas, which is divided up by circles and curves. There is no sense of conventional perspective or even gravity – creating a topsy-turvy world that became characteristic of much of Chagall's work.

Entering the Beehive

A few months after his arrival in Paris, Chagall moved into a studio complex known as *La Ruche*, or the Beehive, which was home to many foreign artists and writers (see pages 14-15). At the same time, he became close friends with a Swiss poet called Blaise Cendrars, who spoke Russian. Cendrars made up titles for some of Chagall's paintings (including *I and the Village*) and introduced the newcomer to significant figures in the modern art world.

'THE SCHOOL OF PARIS'

There was an extraordinary number of foreign artists working in Paris at this time. Despite their different styles, they became known as 'the School of Paris'. By living in La Ruche, Chagall was at the centre of this 'school' yet he maintained his individuality. He continued to draw inspiration from memories and myths of his Russian homeland. Jewish violinists, such as the one featured opposite, appear in many of his pictures.

▲ Blaise Cendrars, c.1914. This widely-travelled poet helped Chagall to settle down in his new surroundings.

▲ *Window*, 1912, Robert Delaunay.

INFLUENTIAL FRIENDS

Among those who befriended the young Chagall when he arrived in Paris were Robert Delaunay (1885-1941) and his wife, Sonia (1895-1979). The couple were well-known figures in the Parisian avant-garde, and Sonia, who was Russian, invited Chagall and other Russian artists to weekend gatherings.

Between 1911 and 1914, the Delaunays developed an off-shoot of Cubism, known as Orphism (or Orphic Cubism), of which *Window* (left) is an example. These terms are derived from Orpheus, a legendary poet and singer in Greek mythology. They were coined by the poet and critic Guillaume Apollinaire (see page 16) to evoke the elements of harmonious lyricism and vibrant colour which the Delaunays injected into Cubism. Chagall also brought geometric shapes and segments of bright colour into his work at this time, as seen both in *I and the Village* (see page 11) and the white triangles and the yellow and green curved 'ground' in *The Fiddler*.

TIMELINE ▶

1912	1913
Chagall exhibits paintings at the Salon des Indépendants and, at the invitation of Delaunay, the Salon d'Automne. Apollinaire introduces him to Berlin art dealer and publisher Herwarth Walden (1878-1941).	Chagall exhibits three pictures at the Salon des Indépendants.

The Fiddler, 1912-13

oil on canvas 188 x 158 cm Stedelijk Museum of Modern Art, Amsterdam

Violinists featured prominently at births, marriages and deaths in traditional Jewish communities, and so became an embodiment of the cycle of life. This is a fiddler on the roof, a symbol of the unstable position of Jews in society.

La Ruche – an artists' colony

Before they achieve financial success – if they ever do – aspiring young artists often need a cheap place to live and paint. In Paris at the beginning of the 20th century, this need was fulfilled for many by a ramshackle cluster of studios known as La Ruche (the Beehive). Situated uncomfortably near the slaughterhouses in a run-down district of Paris known as the Vaurigard, La Ruche was not a sophisticated address, but it was an exciting and conveniently cheap place to live and work.

▲ La Ruche, or the Beehive, in 1968. It is easy to see from its shape how the building got its name. The studios were saved from demolition in the 1960s and are still lived in and worked in today.

SALVAGED STUDIOS

La Ruche was the brainchild of the sculptor and painter Alfred Boucher (1850-1934), a descendant of the great 18th-century Rococo painter François Boucher (1703-70). Boucher bought a plot of land between the railway and the slaughterhouses, and built the studios from pavilions salvaged from the Universal Exhibition that had been held in Paris in 1900. The original building was a twelve-sided, three-story 'beehive' construction, with a cluster of 24 wedge-shaped studios. Eventually there were more than 140 studios on Boucher's plot.

SPACE TO LIVE AND WORK

Boucher wanted to create a community which would provide artists and writers from all over the world with the accommodation and work space they needed for a low rent – 50 to 300 francs per year, according to size. With his grant from Maxim Vinaver of about 125 francs a month, Chagall was able to afford a large studio on the top floor with plenty of light.

Most of the inhabitants of La Ruche were foreigners – Russians, Italians, Germans, Poles and Spaniards. It provided a welcome refuge for Jewish artists in particular who suffered persecution and the threat of pogroms – organised massacres of Jewish communities in Eastern Europe.

FAMOUS NEIGHBOURS

An extraordinary array of artists came to La Ruche, many of whom were to become famous names in 20th-century art. Among Chagall's now celebrated neighbours were the Italian Jew Amedeo Modigliani (1884-1920) and the Lithuanian Jew Chaïm Soutine (1893-1943). There was the painter Fernand Léger (1881-1955) and the sculptors Alexander Archipenko (1887-1964) and Jacques Lipchitz (1891-1973). Many writers, poets and intellectuals came and went too. Even the Russian revolutionary leader Vladimir Ilyich Lenin (1870-1924) stayed at La Ruche for a short time. It was a melting pot of radical ideas about art and politics.

▲ *Max Jacob*, 1916, Amedeo Modigliani. Modigliani created dramatic effects by elongating and simplifying the human face and body.

AN ARTIST'S IMPRESSION

Chagall's own description gives a vivid impression of the atmosphere at La Ruche: 'On the floor, reproductions of El Greco and Cézanne lie cheek by jowl with the remains of a herring... In the Russian studios a slighted model can be heard sobbing, from the Italians comes the sound of guitars and singing, and from the Jews heated discussions. Meanwhile I am quite alone in my studio, working by my petrol lamp... Two, three o'clock in the morning... Somewhere they are slaughtering cattle, the cows are lowing, and I paint them.'

◀ A studio in La Ruche, 1906. The studios' shape was often compared to a wedge of brie cheese.

A growing reputation

▲ World War I is remembered for its trench warfare and the huge loss of life it caused.

WORLD WAR I

In June 1914, around the time that Chagall left Berlin for Vitebsk, Archduke Franz Ferdinand, heir to the throne of Austria-Hungary, was assassinated. Europe was already divided into two armed camps and this event triggered outright war. By August 1914, Austria-Hungary and Germany were at war with France, Russia and Britain. Turkey and Bulgaria later joined the German side. Japan, Italy and the USA came to support Britain, France and Russia. This is the conflict we now know as World War I.

World War I is often called the 'war to end all wars'. No one had anticipated its huge cost nor the vast number of casualties – over 13 million people died. The war's effect on Europe was profound. It triggered the Russian Revolution (see page 22) and left the defeated Germany in economic ruin, so sowing the seeds for World War II and the Holocaust (see page 28).

During his time in Paris, Chagall's self-confidence grew: he was financially secure, his friends acknowledged his talent and his work was gaining recognition. This confidence is expressed in his self-portrait shown here. Chagall, elegantly dressed, works at his easel in his Parisian studio, with the Eiffel Tower seen through the window. His dreams of Russia are shown in a cloud to his right.

The poet and critic Guillaume Apollinaire helped to establish Chagall's reputation in France and abroad. Apollinaire introduced him to the avant-garde Berlin art dealer Herwarth Walden, who was so impressed that he organised a one-man show at his Berlin gallery, Der Sturm.

◄ *Landscape with Cow and Camel*, 1914, August Macke. Macke (1887-1914) was part of *Der Blaue Reiter* (Blue Rider) group. Walden promoted them, and other groups of avant-garde artists, at his Der Sturm gallery.

RETURNING TO RUSSIA

Chagall left Paris in 1914 to attend his Berlin exhibition, which was a great success. He then travelled on to Vitebsk for what he intended to be a short holiday. But world events changed his plans. While he was in Russia, World War I broke out and the Russian borders closed. Chagall was unable to leave. It was nine years before he returned to Paris.

TIMELINE ▶

May 1914	June 1914	August 1914
Chagall arranges to travel to Berlin for his first one-man exhibition at Walden's Der Sturm gallery.	Exhibition opens to good reviews. Chagall travels on to Russia. Archduke Franz Ferdinand of Austria-Hungary is assassinated.	Germany invades France through Belgium. Britain declares war on Germany. World War I has begun. Chagall is stranded in Vitebsk.

Self Portrait with Seven Fingers, 1912-13

oil on canvas 126 x 107 cm Stedelijk Museum of Modern Art, Amsterdam

Chagall shows himself painting an earlier work, *To Russia, Donkeys, and Others*, 1912. Hebrew lettering on the wall above reads 'Paris' and 'Russia'. Why seven fingers? Seven is a mystical number in Jewish symbolism and 'with seven fingers' is a Yiddish expression for working 'at full speed'. Seven also had personal significance for Chagall, as he was born on the seventh day of the seventh month of 1887.

To Russia with love

PRE-REVOLUTIONARY RUSSIA

Before the Bolshevik Revolution of 1917, Russia was a vast empire ruled over by an emperor or Tsar, who had absolute power.

The Russian empire stretched from Germany to the Pacific Ocean, and was made up of many national and ethnic groups. Only half of its 170 million population was actually Russian.

While the Tsar and the nobility lived in luxury, more than 80 per cent of the population were peasants who, until 1861, had been 'serfs'. Serfs were effectively slaves, tied to the land and the property of the landowner. Most of the families who worked on the land lived in terrible poverty. Workers in the cities had similarly miserable living conditions. Understandably, the peasants and workers were open to revolutionary ideas which gave them hope of freedom from this oppression and poverty.

◀ Chagall, his wife Bella and their daughter Ida, 1917. Chagall had returned to Russia partly in order to continue his courtship of Bella. He was uncertain about the welcome he would receive from her but his devotion was amply rewarded.

Back in Vitebsk, Chagall was reunited with his beloved Bella Rosenfeld. She had also just returned home – from Moscow where she had been studying acting. Bella's wealthy parents were not happy about her relationship with a poor, whimsical painter. But the couple were passionately in love, and despite this parental opposition, they married in July 1915. Their mutual love is expressed in many paintings, including *The Birthday*.

RECOGNITION AT HOME

Chagall had to do military service in the war but did not have to fight. His brother-in-law Jacob, an economist, arranged an office job in the War Economy Office in Petrograd (formerly St Petersburg). Chagall moved there, visiting Bella as often as he could. In 1916 and 1917, he exhibited paintings in Petrograd and Moscow. By the time Chagall was 30, much to his pleasure, he was recognised as a major artist. Personal fulfilment also came when, on 18 May 1916, Bella gave birth to their daughter, Ida.

▲ A group of Russian peasants walk to harvest with their scythes in about 1900.

TIMELINE ▶

1915	April 1916	18 May 1916	November 1916
On 25 July Chagall marries Bella Rosenfeld in Vitebsk. He moves to Petrograd to take up a position as a clerk in the press department of the War Economy Office.	Chagall shows 63 recent works in an exhibition of 'Contemporary Russian Art' in Petrograd.	Chagall's daughter Ida is born.	Chagall shows 45 works at an exhibition in Moscow, as part of the avant-garde association of artists exhibiting together under the name of the 'Knave of Diamonds'.

The Birthday, 1915

oil on canvas 81 x 100 cm Museum of Modern Art, New York

In this joyful, dream-like double portrait, Chagall and Bella float above the ground, enraptured by each other's gaze. In her book of memoirs, *First Encounter*, Bella described how she was decorating Chagall's room with shawls and flowers for his birthday, when he told her to stand still so that he could paint her: 'You snatched the brushes, and squeezed out the paint, red, blue, white, transporting me in a stream of colour. United we float over the decorated room, come to the window and want to fly out.'

'She [Bella] has been haunting my paintings, the grand central image of my art.'

Marc Chagall

Chagall the commissar

▲ *Suprematist Composition: White on White,* 1917-18, Kasimir Malevich.

KASIMIR MALEVICH

One of the most radical artists working in revolutionary Russia was Kasimir Malevich (1878-1935), a pioneer of abstract art. He experimented with a number of styles, but wanted to 'free art from the burden of the object', and developed a system of stark geometric abstraction called Suprematism.

Suprematism had a huge influence not just on painting but on commercial art, typography (lettering), furniture design and architecture throughout Europe.

Malevich's most famous picture is *Suprematist Composition: White on White,* 1917-18 (above), a white square tilted on a square white canvas. In its powerful minimalism, it remains an important piece in 20th-century abstract art. Despite criticising Chagall's figurative art, Malevich later adopted a more traditional style.

In 1917, Russian discontent with the war, combined with hatred of the Tsar, led to the Russian Revolution (see page 22). Along with peasants and workers, Jews were given new civil rights. Chagall welcomed the freedom that the revolution seemed to promise. In *The Cemetery Gates* (right), he implies that Jews will reach 'the promised land'.

WORKING FOR THE REVOLUTION

Despite Bella's opposition, the usually apolitical Chagall showed his enthusiasm for the new regime by accepting a job in 1918 as Commissar for the Fine Arts in Vitebsk. He threw himself into his new role, and organised a vast artistic celebration to mark the first anniversary of the Russian Revolution.

◀ The committee of the Vitebsk Academy of Fine Arts, 1919. Chagall sits third from left, his old teacher Yehuda Pen third from right.

In 1919, Chagall opened the Vitebsk Academy of Fine Arts. Naïvely he employed a wide range of artists for the teaching staff, from traditionalists like his old teacher Yehuda Pen to the abstract artist Kasimir Malevich (see panel). Malevich bitterly opposed Chagall and his 'old-fashioned' ideas. While Chagall was away, he took over the school. Angry and hurt, Chagall left Vitebsk for good.

TIMELINE ▶

1917	1918	1919
February and October Revolutions in Russia. Chagall turns down a job as Head of Fine Arts in the new Ministry of Culture. On its own, Russia agrees peace with Germany in November.	First monograph on Chagall is published by Abraham Efross and Jacob Tugendhold. Chagall appointed Commissar for the Fine Arts in Vitebsk. World War I ends.	Chagall opens Vitebsk Academy of Fine Arts. His work is exhibited in two rooms of 'First State Revolutionary Art' at the Winter Palace in Petrograd.

The Cemetery Gates, 1917

oil on canvas 87 x 68.5 cm Centre National d'Art et de Culture Georges Pompidou, Paris, Gift of Ida Chagall

Chagall has written in Hebrew above the gates of the Jewish cemetery the hopeful Old Testament words: 'This saith the Lord God: Behold, O my people, I will open your graves and cause you to come up out of your graves and take you to the land of Israel.' The splintering of the sky and trees into angular planes shows the influence of Cubism.

The Russian Revolution

The Russian Revolution did not happen suddenly. In 1905, protests and strikes had forced the Tsar to form a parliament, or Duma. However, it had little power and the Tsar's regime remained extremely repressive. Illegal opposition groups operated in secret. The largest of these was the Social Democratic Party, which followed the teachings of Karl Marx (1818-83). He believed there should be a socialist revolution where the wealth of the country would be shared among the people.

▲ The Russian royal family with Tsar Nicholas at its centre. The Tsar's failure to make meaningful reforms led to revolution and the eventual death of him and his family in 1918. They were shot, in secret, by the Bolshevik Red Guards.

RUSSIA AT WAR

Opposition to the Tsar grew after Russia's disastrous role in World War I. Bad leadership and organisation led to terrible losses with casualties running to millions. The war put a great strain on the Russian economy, and riots began over food shortages. In March 1917, Tsar Nicholas sent troops to put down riots in Petrograd, but the soldiers mutinied and joined the protesters. The Tsar abdicated, and the Duma formed a Provisional Government. These events are referred to as the 'February Revolution'.

THE BOLSHEVIKS EMERGE

The new government was moderate politically, and had to face challenges from the soviets or workers

A NOTE ON DATES

At the time of the Russian Revolution, Russia still used the old-style calendar, which was 13 days behind the Western-style calendar we use today (the Gregorian calendar). This means – rather confusingly – that the Revolutions usually referred to as the 'February' and 'October' Revolutions took place in March and November 1917 respectively.

◀ Russian casualties in World War I were so bad that the army was forced to use child soldiers. Many, like this one here, were taken prisoner by the Germans.

councils. The government could not solve Russia's economic crisis, largely because it carried on the war, and it became more and more unpopular. With the Tsar gone, there was political freedom, which enabled a radical wing of the Social Democratic Party – the Bolsheviks – to gain popularity.

ALL POWER TO THE SOVIETS

The Bolshevik leader Vladimir Ilyich Lenin led the opposition to the Provisional Government, rallying support with the slogan 'Peace! Bread! Land! All power to the soviets!' On 6 November 1917, Bolshevik troops stormed the Winter Palace and seized power. Lenin quickly established a new government, and began radical changes to Russian society: titles and rank were abolished; peasants were given the right to take land; women were given equal rights with men.

COMMUNIST RULE

However, the future of the Russian people was far from bright. When the Bolshevik party failed to gain many votes in the elections in November, Lenin gave up the idea of parliamentary democracy. The communists (as the Bolsheviks now called themselves) would rule as a dictatorship. Their regime would eventually be as repressive as that of the tsars'.

The new communist government made peace with Germany, but gave up a lot of territory and resources in the peace treaty. Soon, discontent with communist rule led to a terrible civil war. The communists won in 1921, but Russia's economy was in ruins. The ordinary workers and peasants continued to suffer as much as ever.

In 1922, the year in which Chagall left Russia for good, the country became the Union of Soviet Socialist Republics (USSR).

◀ This Communist poster, created after 1922, shows the hammer and sickle – symbols of the urban workers and rural peasants. They were combined to become the symbol of the USSR. Lenin, the first leader of the USSR, is also shown (top left).

Disapproval and departure

▲ *The Drowned Woman*, 1928, Marc Chagall. Chagall initially painted this illustration for one of La Fontaine's *Fables* in gouache. Later this was used to make an etching.

ILLUSTRATIONS AND ETCHINGS

Back in France, Chagall took on several commissions from the art dealer and publisher Ambroise Vollard (1866-1939). These commissions not only gave Chagall some income, but enabled him to develop his etching technique, which he had begun to do in Berlin. One of the projects was illustrating the *Fables* of La Fontaine (1621-95). For this, Chagall initially created the images with gouache, which he particularly liked. These were later engraved on to copper plates to be printed in a book of limited-edition etchings; Chagall hand-finished all 8,500 prints in colour.

In May 1920, Chagall and his family moved to Moscow, where he painted a series of huge murals for the State Jewish Chamber Theatre. Dancers, musicians, actors, acrobats, fiddlers, traditional Jewish figures – and Chagall himself – were shown cavorting against a geometric background. Chagall considered it among his best work, but the communist authorities disapproved, seeing it as self-indulgent and irrelevant to Russian society. They refused to pay him and, despite his fame, sidelined him into a lowly job, teaching drawing to war orphans. Chagall decided to leave the country.

▶ Chagall teaching in an orphan colony in Russia. Despite the job's lowly status, Chagall 'delighted' in the children's drawings.

STOLEN WORKS OF ART

After spending a year in Berlin, in 1923 Chagall took his family back to France, where he stayed for almost 20 years. In both Berlin and Paris he was devastated to find that many of the early works, which had brought him fame, had been stolen or lost. Initially, he painted replicas to replace them. As he settled down, he began to explore France and to experiment with new techniques. The sense of peace he enjoyed is expressed in *The Acrobat* (right).

TIMELINE ▶

1920	1921	1922	1923	1926
Chagall leaves Vitebsk for Moscow. He paints murals for Moscow's Jewish Theatre.	Chagall teaches drawing to war orphans. He begins his autobiography.	Chagall and family leave Russia for Berlin. He makes 20 etchings for his autobiography.	Chagall returns to Paris. He paints numerous replicas and variants of early works that were lost in his absence.	Chagall's first solo show is organised in the USA at the Reinhardt Gallery in New York. He begins work on illustrations for La Fontaine's *Fables*.

The Acrobat, 1930

oil on canvas 117 x 73.5 cm
Centre National d'Art et
de Culture Georges
Pompidou, Paris

In 1927, after the two
friends had been to the
Winter Circus in Paris
together, Ambroise Vollard
commissioned Chagall to do
a series of 19 gouaches on
a circus theme. The subject
became a favourite for
Chagall. His circus pictures
are touched with a moving
sense of magic, poetry and
personal drama. The
dreaminess of this charming
image is accentuated by a
softer, blurred technique.

*'I always regarded clowns, acrobats and actors as tragic figures,
which for me resemble the figures in religious paintings.'*

Marc Chagall

Visiting the Holy Land

▲ Chagall shortly after the publication of his autobiography, *My Life*. Bella and Chagall worked closely together on the French edition of the book, discussing the translation from Yiddish line by line.

THE ARTIST'S AUTOBIOGRAPHY

In 1931, the same year the Chagalls visited Palestine, Chagall's autobiography, *Ma Vie* (*My Life*) was published. It had taken ten years to come together. Chagall had begun writing it in Russia and taken it to Berlin in 1922. Here, the art publisher Paul Cassirer (1871-1926) suggested that he publish it in German, and illustrate it with etchings. Although Cassirer produced a printed edition of the 20 etchings of scenes from Chagall's youth, the book itself proved difficult to translate, which is why it was not published until 1931. It was translated from the original Yiddish (Jewish) by Bella Chagall and a young writer Jean Paulhan (1884-1968). An English version was published in 1965.

With the work for his autobiography (see panel), the *Fables* and other projects, Chagall had mastered the art of etching and made it his own. Vollard was so impressed that he gave Chagall an even more important commission – to illustrate the Bible.

A BIBLICAL LANDSCAPE

Chagall had always been fascinated by the Bible. Now he wanted to gain first-hand experience of the biblical homeland of the Jews. Invited by the mayor of Tel Aviv, Chagall and his family set off for the Holy Land early in 1931. They travelled via Egypt and the Lebanon to spend several months in Palestine (Israel did not then exist as a country).

Chagall was inspired by his visit. It sparked off many works, such as *Solitude* (right) in addition to his Bible illustrations. However, the Bible project itself was interrupted by World War II and would not be ready for publication until 1956.

▲ The rocky landscape of the Holy Land is very dramatic. Chagall was inspired by seeing Biblical holy places at first hand.

TIMELINE ▶

1930	1931	1932	1933	1934
Commissioned by Vollard, Chagall starts to illustrate the Bible.	Chagall spends three months in Palestine. His autobiography, *Ma Vie* is published.	Chagall's first exhibition in the Netherlands. He travels to Amsterdam.	A number of Chagall's works are publicly burned by the Nazis.	Chagall travels around Spain.

Solitude, 1933-34

oil on canvas 96 x 158 cm Tel Aviv Museum of Art, Israel

In this sombre, atmospheric painting, familiar motifs in Chagall's art – the placid cow, the fiddle and Russian houses – surround a huge, pensive figure of a traditional Jew, lost in thought as he clutches a Torah scroll (the most sacred text of the Jews). A little white angel flies against a pale blue sky. The figure of the Jew is isolated, exiled like the Jews of Europe. Chagall donated the painting to the Tel Aviv Museum of Art.

'Will God or someone else give me the strength
to breathe the breath of prayer and mourning
into my paintings, the breath of prayer
for redemption and resurrection?'

Marc Chagall, My Life

Tensions in Europe

▲ Jews in Poland are rounded up by German soldiers in 1943.

NAZI ANTI-SEMITISM

Adolf Hitler (1889-1945) and the Nazi (National Socialist) party came to power in Germany in 1933, when the country was in a deep economic depression. Hitler blamed most of Germany's problems on the Jewish people, and his government was dedicated to the persecution of the Jews.

First Jews were banned from the civil service and journalism, then excluded from the armed forces and higher education. By 1938, when Chagall painted *The White Crucifixion*, the Nazi policy became even more repressive and violent, with the Jews being confined to concentration camps and used as forced labour. Then in 1941, under the cover of World War II, the Nazis began simply to kill Jews in a planned extermination which became known as the Holocaust. By 1945, six million Jews, three-quarters of all the Jews in Europe, had been murdered.

In 1935, Chagall travelled to Vilnius (then in Poland, now the capital of Lithuania), where he was guest of honour at the opening of the Jewish Cultural Institute. He returned to France via Warsaw.

HATRED OF THE JEWS

The visit to Poland made Chagall very aware of the rise of anti-Semitism (anti-Jewish feelings) in Europe, particularly in Nazi Germany (see panel). By the mid-1930s, Nazi anti-Semitism affected Chagall personally. All his works were removed from German museums and in 1937 – the year in which Chagall became a French citizen – three of them were shown in the Nazis' Degenerate Art exhibition.

▲ This illustration shows the Nazis' Degenerate Art exhibition held in 1937. Its aim was to ridicule art that did not conform with Nazi beliefs.

A CRY OF PROTEST

The White Crucifixion was painted in 1938. It was Chagall's reaction to the Nazi persecution of the Jewish people. Some Jews were offended by his use of Christian imagery but Chagall saw Jesus, himself a Jew, as a symbol of all suffering Jews.

TIMELINE ▶

1935	1937	1938
Chagall travels to Vilnius, then in Poland (now in Lithuania). He visits Warsaw and sees the threat to the Jewish population.	Chagall travels to Italy. All his works are removed from German museums by the Nazis and three are shown at the Degenerate Art Exhibition. Chagall becomes a French citizen.	Chagall exhibits in Brussels. He paints *The White Crucifixion*.

The White Crucifixion, 1938

oil on canvas 154.3 x 139.7 cm The Art Institute of Chicago

Around the central figure of the crucified Christ, Chagall has painted a variety of scenes that show Jewish
suffering. A village is attacked and burned by Nazi soldiers; all around are frightened, fleeing or
lamenting Jewish figures. A wandering Jew clutching a Torah symbolises the homeless Jews as in *Solitude*
(see page 27). There is also a burning Torah (bottom right). In the early 1930s, Chagall had travelled
round Europe and seen many paintings by the Old Masters, for whom the crucifixion was a standard
subject. By borrowing a central image from traditional Christian art, Chagall perhaps indicates that the
persecution of the Jews is a universal outrage that affects everyone, regardless of their religion or race.

Exile in America

ARTISTS IN EXILE

Many artists, writers, composers and intellectuals fled Europe, particularly occupied France, during World War II. Many found a safe haven in New York, as Chagall did.

These European artists were warmly welcomed and a number of exhibitions were held in their honour. At his New York gallery, Pierre Matisse (1899-1989, son of the artist Henri Matisse), organised the 'Artists in Exile' exhibition. He gave Chagall, among others, several one-man shows. In addition, the Museum of Modern Art put on an 'Art in Exile' exhibition, while the Whitney Museum held an exhibition called 'European Artists in America'.

▲ This 1940s' postcard conveys the excitement of New York through its famous skyline, with the Empire State Building in the centre.

When World War II began in 1939, the Chagalls were living outside Paris. In 1940 they moved to the South of France, arriving in the village of Gordes at the same time as the German army occupied Paris. They lived there for about a year, but like all Jews in France, they were in danger of being caught and taken to a concentration camp. Luckily help was at hand. The Museum of Modern Art in New York sent Chagall an invitation to come to the United States.

LEAVING FRANCE

On 23 June 1941, the Chagalls sailed into New York. They brought with them Chagall's work packed up in crates and trunks. He was determined never again to suffer the loss of his work as had happened in 1914 (see page 24).

Despite not speaking English, Chagall was soon happily settled in New York. A one-man show of his work received rave reviews (see panel) and commissions for theatre and ballet designs followed. During this period, Chagall painted a number of canvases showing horrific scenes of war, but also painted more optimistic images such as *The Juggler* (right).

▲ Chagall's first exhibition at the Pierre Matisse Gallery, New York, 1941.

TIMELINE ▶

1939	1940	1941	1942
Shortly before the outbreak of World War II in September, Chagall and his family leave Paris for the Loire Valley.	The Chagalls move further south to Gordes in the Vaucluse mountains. Chagall receives an invitation to go to the USA from the Museum of Modern Art in New York.	The Chagalls leave France. Chagall has his first US exhibition at Pierre Matisse's gallery in New York.	Chagall spends the summer in Mexico, working on ballet designs.

The Juggler, 1943

oil on canvas 109.9 x 79.1 cm The Art Institute of Chicago

Part man, part bird, part angel, the flamboyant central figure dances in a circus ring, a clock (a traditional symbol of time passing and the inevitability of death) draped over one arm. Old Russian houses and a Jewish fiddler are among the secondary scenes. As usual with Chagall, it is impossible to read the symbolism precisely, but the painting seems to express the energy and variety of the human spirit.

New York immigrants

When Marc Chagall sailed into New York harbour, he became one of the millions of immigrants who had fled poverty or persecution to find a new life in the USA. For the Chagalls, and for millions of others, the first sight that greeted them was the Statue of Liberty, towering above the water, her plinth inscribed with these idealistic, welcoming words: 'Give me your tired, your poor... Your huddled masses, yearning to breathe free.'

FIRST STOP – ELLIS ISLAND

Near to Liberty Island, where the statue stands, is Ellis Island. Until 1954, this was where immigrants to the USA made their first stop, at the immigration centre. They were interviewed and given medical checks before being admitted into the country. Some had to endure weeks or even months of waiting. In its 62-year history, 12 million immigrants passed through Ellis Island.

▲ Immigrants to the USA on board a ship, c. 1915, cheer and throw up their hats as they see the Statue of Liberty.

In the 19th and early 20th centuries, huge numbers of immigrants arrived in the USA – from South and Central America, Europe, Russia and eastern Asia. On Ellis Island, once they had been permitted entry, they could buy cheap train tickets which allowed them to travel on to cities such as Chicago and San Francisco.

▼ Immigrants queue at Ellis Island, c. 1905, waiting to be admitted into the USA and a new life.

▲ By 1898, when this picture was taken, the Jewish community was well-established in the Lower East Side of New York. In this crowded Orchard Street market, some of the signs hanging from storefronts are written in Hebrew.

STICKING TOGETHER

Many immigrants chose to stay in New York, and the city became a rich mix of cultures. National and regional groups tended to move into the same areas, as the names Chinatown and Little Italy imply.

Around the time of Chagall's birth, the first boatloads of Eastern European immigrants were settling in the crowded streets of the Lower East Side of Manhattan. Between 1870 and 1920, when new immigration laws reduced the numbers, millions of Russians, Slavs, Poles and Lithuanians settled here. Often two or three families would share an apartment in the five-storey tenement blocks. This became the Jewish centre of the city, where Yiddish was the language most spoken, and where at one time there were 500 synagogues.

'I am impressed by the greatness of this country [America] and the feeling of freedom that it gives me.'

Marc Chagall

HOME FROM HOME

Chagall, who never learned English but always spoke Yiddish, Russian or French, felt at home on the Lower East Side. He loved the Jewish food and the Yiddish newspapers he could buy. By now, however, he was wealthy, and could afford to live in a more up-market area. At first he and Bella stayed in hotels, but to have the peace and space to paint, they moved to an apartment on 74th Street on Manhattan's Upper West Side.

The death of Bella

▲ Ida Chagall in 1945. She is standing beside one of her father's paintings of her mother, *My Fiancée in Black Gloves*, 1909.

IDA CHAGALL (1916-94)

Bella and Marc Chagall's only child Ida had a very close relationship with her father. In her adult years, she was dedicated to supporting him, and promoting his international reputation. She handled his business affairs, organised exhibitions and liaised with journalists and publishers. She even sewed the costumes for his stage designs – as her mother had done before her.

In 1934, aged 18, she married a young lawyer Michel Gorday, but the couple later divorced. In 1952, she married the art historian Franz Meyer who wrote an important study of Chagall. Apparently something of a matchmaker, she was responsible for introducing her father to the two women in his life following Bella's death – Virginia Haggard and Valentina (Vava) Brodsky (see page 36).

The Chagalls sometimes left the city to stay in the country at Cranberry Lake in upstate New York. While here they heard that Paris had been liberated from the Nazis, on 25 August 1944. Bella felt lonely in New York, and was looking forward to returning to Paris. But it was not to be. On 2 September 1944 she died suddenly of an infection.

Chagall was devastated. 'Everything has grown dark before my eyes,' he wrote. Their daughter, Ida, brought him to live with her at her New York apartment. He turned his canvases to the wall, and for nine months painted nothing.

FINDING NEW PURPOSE

Eventually, Chagall moved back into his own home and began to work again. He was painting *Around Her* (right) when he met Virginia Haggard McNeil, whom Ida had arranged to be his housekeeper. The two gradually fell in love and were together for seven years. They had a son, David, but their relationship was not known about publicly until after Chagall's death.

◀ This photograph of Chagall with Virginia and their son in 1951 appeared in *My Life with Chagall, Seven Years of Plenty*. This revealing book was written by Virginia and published in 1986, the year after Chagall's death.

Around Her, 1945

oil on canvas 131 x 109.7 cm Centre National d'Art et de Culture Georges Pompidou, Paris

Here Chagall's blues, usually so rich and vibrant, are dark and muted, reflecting the bereaved artist's sadness. Bella weeps quietly (right), while Chagall paints. His head – like his world – is turned upside down. The images form a circular movement, an acrobat swoops down, the bridal couple fly up, and a crystal ball at the centre reveals memories of Vitebsk.

Vava and Vence

In 1963 the French government invited Chagall to paint the ceiling of the Paris Opéra. Some critics objected to the idea of a Russian Jew decorating this French national monument, while others thought that modern art was wrong for a 19th-century building. But nearly everyone agreed that the result was a masterpiece.

It was a huge undertaking: Chagall painted over 220 square metres of canvas, which were glued to panels of polyester and then hoisted to the ceiling. Once the panels were in position, the 77-year-old artist climbed 23 metres of scaffolding to reach the ceiling and touch up details. When the ceiling painting was first seen on 23 September 1964, one critic wrote: 'For once, the best seats in the house were in the uppermost circle.'

After seven years in the United States, Chagall was ready to return to France. In 1948, he and Virginia moved into a house outside Paris, but also travelled to Italy and the Côte d'Azur in the South of France, where Picasso and Matisse were living. Chagall loved the Côte d'Azur, and in 1950, he bought 'La Colline', a beautiful house with a huge studio overlooking the Mediterranean at Vence.

In 1951, Chagall and Virginia separated. The following year Ida introduced her father to a young Russian Valentina Brodsky (Vava). In July 1952, they married.

▶ Chagall with Vava in 1962. They remained happily together until Chagall's death. At Vava's request, Chagall's relationship with Virginia was never made public.

▲ The ceiling of the Paris Opéra, 1964.

MONUMENTAL WORK

From the 1950s onwards, Chagall often worked on a monumental scale, including projects like the Paris Opéra (see panel). He discovered a run-down chapel in Vence, and spent some 20 years on a series of vast paintings called the 'Biblical Messsage' intended for it. When it proved impossible to install the paintings in the chapel, Chagall donated them to the city of Nice, where a museum was opened in 1973 to house them.

TIMELINE ▶

1948	1950	1951	1952	1955	1956	1957	1964
Chagall returns to live in France, initially outside Paris.	Chagall moves to Vence. He meets lithographer Charles Sorlier.	Chagall exhibits in Israel. He separates from Virginia Haggard.	Chagall meets Valentina Brodsky (Vava), whom he marries on 12 July.	Chagall begins 'Biblical Message' paintings.	Chagall's Bible etchings finally published.	Designs wall mosaics and stained-glass windows.	Chagall paints the ceiling of the Paris Opéra.

Abraham and the Three Angels, 1960-66
oil on canvas 190 x 292 cm Musée National Message Biblique, Nice

Almost three metres long, this magnificent canvas is one of the paintings in the Biblical Message series. There were seventeen pictures in the series, featuring episodes from three different biblical books: Genesis, Exodus and the Song of Solomon. This scene shows the episode in Genesis where Abraham gives hospitality – rest, food and drink – to three angels of God. In return, they promise him that his wife, Sarah, will conceive a child, despite her age. Painted when Chagall was in his seventies, it shows the striking vibrancy of colour and poetic power that characterise his work throughout his life.

'Ever since early childhood, I have been captivated by the Bible. It has always seemed to me, and still seems today, the greatest source of poetry imaginable.'

Marc Chagall

A productive old age

◀ **The Artist in his Studio, 1976.** Chagall produced about 1,100 lithographs like this one during his career.

Chagall's late years were remarkably productive: as well as painting, he made lithographs, stained-glass windows, monumental mosaics, ceramics, sculptures and tapestries. He was applauded as one of the greatest living artists of the 20th century.

RETURNING TO RUSSIA

In 1973, Chagall, aged 86, was invited by the Soviet Culture Minister to visit Russia. It was the first time he had returned there since 1922. The authorities organised an exhibition in Moscow to celebrate the event, at which Chagall was asked to sign the murals for the Jewish Theatre rejected 50 years before (see page 24). The old Russian artist was moved to tears.

Major exhibitions of Chagall's work continued to be held through the 1980s, including one at London's Royal Academy. The 97-year-old Chagall was too frail to attend its opening in January 1985. Two months later, on the evening of 28 March, after spending all day at work on a lithograph, he died peacefully of old age.

LITHOGRAPHY

Lithography is a printing technique where the image is originally drawn or painted on stone. Chagall produced more than a thousand lithographs. For many years, from 1950 until his death, he worked closely with expert lithographer Charles Sorlier. Sorlier prepared the lithographic stones for Chagall, eventually replacing the traditional limestone plates with copper ones.

Before he met Sorlier (who became like a son to him), Chagall had made only black-and-white lithographs, but Sorlier had the technical expertise to allow him to bring his glorious sense of colour to the medium. Indeed, the brilliant colour Chagall achieved in lithography seems to have had an effect on his use of colour in paintings and stained-glass.

◀ **Chagall signs autographs for the admirers that surround him in Moscow, 1973.**

TIMELINE ▶

1966	1969	1973	1977	28 March 1985
Chagall and Vava move to Saint-Paul-de-Vence.	Foundation stone for Biblical Message museum laid. 'Hommáge a Marc Chagall' exhibition of 474 works at Grand Palais in Paris.	Chagall visits Russia for the first time in 50 years. Reunited with two of his sisters.	Chagall is awarded France's highest honour, the Grand Cross of the Legion of Honour. Chagall exhibition at the Louvre: the first ever for a living artist.	Chagall dies at his home in Saint-Paul-de-Vence.

> *'There is something very simple about a stained-glass window: just materials and light.'*
>
> *Marc Chagall*

The Arts to the Glory of God, 1978

stained glass window 317.5 x 138.4 cm Chichester Cathedral, West Sussex

Chagall did not even begin to make stained-glass windows until he was almost 70, yet he is acknowledged – along with Matisse – as one of the 20th-century masters of this particular art form. This window for Chichester Cathedral was completed when Chagall was over 90 years old. It takes its inspiration from Psalm 150 and is usually described by the Psalm's last line, 'Let everything that hath breath, praise the Lord'. Stained glass is a particularly appropriate medium for Chagall. The effect of light shining through coloured glass is close to the luminous quality he strived to achieve in his painting.

Chagall's legacy

Marc Chagall was buried in the Catholic cemetery in Saint-Paul-de-Vence, the village where he died. Some protested that he should have been buried in a Jewish cemetery, but this contradiction is just one of many that makes up the artist Chagall. He was a Russian and a Frenchman; a Jew who held many beliefs that were not Jewish.

These contradictions can be found in his work: in the cultural mix of his imagery; in the sense of joy that is often tinged with sadness; in the harmonious order he creates from his jumble of subjects. It is this perhaps that makes his art so universally popular. In his struggle to create a new reality which embraces all these contradictions, Chagall reflects the struggle we all face, but gives us hope in the sense of celebration and unity he achieves.

> *'In the arts, as in life, everything is possible provided it is based on love.'*
>
> Marc Chagall

▲ *Son of Man*, 1964, René Magritte. One of the Surrealists, Magritte (1898-1967) uses images like the bowler hat again and again, like the repeated images in Chagall's work.

▲ Chagall's mosaic *The Prophet Elijah* at the Biblical Message Museum in Nice. Chagall felt the work was relevant to everyone, regardless of their religious beliefs.

WORKING APART

Chagall remained outside the major art movements of the 20th century. He flirted with Cubism and Orphism but always kept his own unique style. In the 1920s, Chagall was asked and refused to join the Surrealists. This group of artists and writers aimed to express the world of dreams and the unconscious mind. To do this the Surrealists often used everyday objects as symbols, or metaphors, of ideas, something Chagall had done before them. Surrealism's founder André Breton (1896-1966) recognised Chagall's influence, writing that, through him, 'metaphor made its triumphant entry into modern painting'.

▶ *Life*, c. 1990, Yvette Cauquil-Prince. This magnificent tapestry was produced some five years after Chagall's death. In it many of his favourite themes can be seen – circus performers, loving couples, musicians – pictured on a dramatic scale. The huge tapestry measures 361 x 485 cm.

ART AND CRAFT

In his later years, Chagall embarked on many projects – in stained-glass, lithography and tapestry – which required the technical skills of crafts people. One such person was master-craftswoman Yvette Cauquil-Prince (b. 1928), a tapestry maker whom Chagall met in 1964. She had been producing tapestries based on art works by many 20th-century masters. Chagall collaborated with her and she continued to produce tapestries from his designs even after his death. Although the images already existed in other forms, the different technique and the huge change in scale meant that an entirely new work of art was created, giving new life to Chagall's work.

STILL IN THE SPOTLIGHT

Chagall's work continues to find new admirers today. Greeting cards and posters of his hugely popular works sell in their thousands. The original art can be seen in museums and galleries around the world – as well as in many other public places: in cathedrals and synagogues, government buildings, theatres and universities. In all these ways people continue to enjoy Chagall's own unique vision of life in all its variety.

'A poet with the wings of a painter.'
Novelist Henry Miller talking about Chagall

◀ Chagall with Yvette Cauquil-Prince, c. 1966.

Poems between friends

Chagall has been described as a 'poet with the wings of a painter', because his whole approach to art has a poetic quality. This may be one of the reasons why many of his friends were poets. Chagall himself wrote poetry. Indeed, his prose and even his way of talking were poetic – full of images and colourful, evocative language.

▼ *My Land*, 1946, by Marc Chagall. These are extracts from a poem Chagall wrote soon after the end of World War II.

Only that land is mine
That lies in my soul.
As a native, with no documents
I enter that land...

Gardens are blooming inside me,
My flowers I invented,
My own streets -
But there are no houses.
They have been destroyed since my childhood.
Their inhabitants stray in the air,
Seek a dwelling,
They live in my soul...

DEDICATED TO CHAGALL

A number of Chagall's poet friends wrote poems to and about him, both in his early years as a struggling young artist in Paris, and later. When he was living at La Ruche (see pages 12-15), he became close to the poet Blaise Cendrars, who dedicated several poems to Chagall, including *Portrait* (below).

He's asleep
He wakes up
Suddenly, he paints
He takes a church and paints
with a church
He takes a cow and paints
with a cow
With a sardine
With heads, hands, knives...

Chagall is astonished to still
be alive.

▲ Extract from *Portrait*, 1913, by Blaise Cendrars.

TIMELINE ▶

1887	1909	1914	1916	1919
7 July Moyshe Segal (Marc Chagall) born in Vitebsk.	**1909** Enrols at Zvantseva School. He meets Bella Rosenfeld, his future wife.	**May** Travels to Berlin for his first one-man exhibition at Der Sturm gallery.	**18 May** Ida Chagall born.	**1919** Opens Vitebsk Academy of Fine Arts.
1906 Enters Yehuda Pen's art school in Vitebsk.	**1910** Moves to Paris. Sees modern French art for first time.	**June** Exhibition opens to good reviews. Chagall travels on to Russia.	**November** Exhibits in Moscow with the avant-garde association of artists, 'Knave of Diamonds'.	**1920** Leaves Vitebsk for Moscow. Paints murals for Moscow's Jewish Theatre.
Winter 1906-7 Moves to St Petersburg.	**1911** Moves into the artists' colony La Ruche (the Beehive). Meets the poets Blaise Cendrars and Guillaume Apollinaire.	**August** World War I has begun. Chagall stranded in Vitebsk.	**1917** Russian Revolution. Chagall turns down job offer as Head of Fine Arts in the new Ministry of Culture.	**1921** Teaches drawing to war orphans. Begins his autobiography.
1907 Enrols in School of the Imperial Society for the Protection of the Fine Arts.		**1915** Marries Bella in Vitebsk on 25 July. Works at the War Economy Office in Petrograd.	**1918** Appointed Commissar for the Fine Arts in Vitebsk. World War I ends.	**1922** Chagall family leave Russia for Berlin. He makes etchings for autobiography.
1908 Leaves the Imperial Society school. Meets Maxim Vinaver.	**1912-13** Has paintings exhibited in Paris.			**1923** Returns to Paris.

Your scarlet face your biplane convertible
*   into hydroplane*
Your round house where a smoked
*   herring swims...*

And I began to cry reminiscing over our
*   childhoods*
And you show me a dreadful purple
This little painting where there is a cart
*   which reminded me of the day*
A day made out of pieces of mauves yellows
*   blues greens and reds...*
Two gold rings near some sandals
Kindle the sun
While your hair is like the trolley cable
Across Europe arrayed in little many-
*   coloured fires.*

◀ **Extract from** *Rotsoge*, **for the painter Marc Chagall, 1914 by Guillaume Apollinaire.**

▼ *To Marc Chagall*, **1950, by Paul Éluard.**

POETRY INSPIRED BY PAINTING

While living at La Ruche, Chagall also met the poet and critic Guillaume Apollinaire, who was a leading figure in the avant-garde and a passionate supporter of Cubism. Chagall was worried that Apollinaire would not like his work, but when the poet visited the artist's studio, he apparently murmured 'Supernatural'. He wrote to Chagall the next day, enclosing the poem above. Later, another poet, Paul Éluard (1895-1952), a leading figure in the Surrealists, was also inspired by Chagall's art (right).

Donkey or cow cock or horse
Even the shell of a violin
A singing man a single bird
Agile dancing man with woman

A couple drenched in its
*   own spring*

Gold of grass lead of sky
Separated by blue flames
A little health a little dew
Rainbowed blood and
*   tolling heart*

A couple the first gleam of day

Catacombed beneath the snow
A vine in opulence outlines
A countenance with lips of moon
That has not ever slept at night.

1926	1937	1946	1952	1969
1926 First US solo show. Begins work on illustrations for La Fontaine's *Fables*.	**1937** Works shown at the Degenerate Art Exhibition. Becomes a French citizen.	**1946** Museum of Modern Art in New York hold retrospective. On 22 June, son David born.	**1952** Meets and marries Valentina Brodsky (Vava).	**1969** Work begins on Biblical Message museum.
1930 Begins work on illustrating the Bible.	**1939** World War II begins.	**1947** Retrospectives held in Paris, Amsterdam, London, Zürich and Berne.	**1955** Begins 'Biblical Message' paintings.	**1973** Chagall visits Russia for first time in 50 years.
1931 Spends three months in Palestine.	**1941** Leaves France for USA. Exhibition at Pierre Matisse's gallery, New York.	**1948** Returns to live in France.	**1956** Bible etchings finally published.	**1977** Awarded France's highest honour, the Grand Cross of the Legion of Honour. Given exhibition at Louvre – the first ever of a living artist.
1933 His autobiography, *Ma Vie*, is published.	**1944** Bella dies suddenly.	**1950** Moves to Vence.	**1957** Designs his first stained-glass window.	
1934 Travels in Spain.	**1945** World War II ends. Meets Virginia Haggard. Designs for Stravinsky's ballet *The Firebird*.	**1951** Travels to Israel. Separates from Virginia.	**1964** Paints the ceiling of the Paris Opéra.	**28 March 1985** Chagall dies at his home in Saint-Paul-de-Vence.
1935 Travels to Poland. Sees threat to European Jews.			**1966** Moves short distance to Saint-Paul-de-Vence.	

Glossary

Abstract art: a style of painting or drawing that creates pictures that are independent of reality; such pictures may sometimes be based on a landscape, person, or some other object seen in the real world, but are made up of colours and lines used for their own sake.

avant-garde: describes new, experimental or radical ideas. From the French for vanguard, the first troops into battle.

Blue Rider, The: a group of Expressionists formed in 1911. The members, who included Wassily Kandinsky (1866-1944), Paul Klee (1879-1940), Franz Marc (1880-1916) and August Macke (1887-1914), had different artistic styles. But they were united in their attempts to use colour in a new way, and to capture a spiritual value in their work.

Bolshevik: a member of the Russian Communist Party, often used for communists generally.

Cubism: the name of an art movement based in Paris from about 1907, led by Pablo Picasso and Georges Braque. The Cubists painted multiple viewpoints of people or objects so they could all be seen at once.

degenerate: something that has descended to a low moral, mental or artistic level.

empire: a large number of countries ruled by a more powerful country.

etching: a print on paper made from an engraved metal plate.

Expressionism: an approach to painting which communicates an emotional state of mind rather than external reality.

Fauves: French for 'wild beasts', the name given by a shocked critic in 1905 to a group of painters, including Henri Matisse (1869-1954) and Andre Derain (1880-1954), who used bright, unnatural colours in their art.

gouache: opaque (non-transparent) watercolour.

lithograph: a print on paper made from a special stone on which an image has been drawn or painted.

minimalist: using extremely simple, abstract forms.

Orphism: an art movement that developed out of Cubism in the early 20th century, led by the French painter Robert Delaunay (1885-1941). It was characterised by a more vibrant use of colour.

palette: a flat board on which artists arrange their oil paints ready for use. Also, the range of colours used in painting.

patron: someone who supports an artist financially by buying their work or giving them money.

portrait: an image of a person's face, which sometimes tries to capture something of their personality.

retrospective: an exhibition showing the development of an artist's work over his or her lifetime.

Rococo: a style of art that emerged in France in the early 18th century. It was characterised by light brushstrokes and playful imagery. François Boucher was one of the greatest Rococo artists.

Salon: annual art exhibition organised by the French Academy. In the 19th century the jury refused works by many Impressionist and Post-Impressionist painters who then exhibited at the Salon des Refusés. The Salon des Indépendants was started in 1884.

Suprematism: a highly influential, if short-lived, Russian art movement started by Kasimir Malevich in 1915. Paintings were abstract, made up of pure geometric shapes – the square, circle, rectangle and triangle.

Surrealism: an intellectual movement that began in the 1920s, which tried to show the life of our unconscious minds and dreams. Its most famous artist is Salvador Dalí (1904-89), but it also included writers and film-makers.

symbols: something, such as an image of an object, that represents something else, such as an idea or an emotion.

Museums and galleries

Works by Chagall are exhibited in museums, galleries and in some special buildings all around the world. Even if you can't visit any of them yourself, you may be able to visit their websites. Gallery websites often show pictures of the artworks they have on display. Some of the websites even offer virtual tours which allow you to wander around and look at different paintings while sitting comfortably in front of your computer!

Most of the international websites detailed below include an option that allows you to view them in English.

EUROPE

Centre National d'Art et de Culture Georges Pompidou
75191 Paris
cedex 04
France
www.centrepompidou.fr

Chichester Cathedral
The Royal Chantry
Cathedral Cloisters
Chichester, West Sussex
PO19 1PX
England
www.fransnet.clara.net/chicath

Kunstmuseum, Berne
Sammlung Im Obersteg
Wichterheer-Gut Staatsstrasse
CH-3653
Switzerland
www.kunstmuseumbern.ch

Musée National Message Biblique Marc Chagall
Avenue Docteur
Ménard 06000
Nice, France
www.ac-nice.fr/chagall/chagall/htm

Stedelijk Museum
Paulus Potterstraat 13
1071 CX Amsterdam
Post Box 75082
1070 AB Amsterdam
The Netherlands
www.stedelijk.nl

USA

Art Institute of Chicago
111 South Michigan Avenue
Chicago, Illinois
IL 60603-6110
www.artic.edu

Museum of Modern Art
33 Street at Queens Blvd
Long Island City,
Queens, New York
www.moma.org

Philadelphia Museum of Art
Benjamin Franklin Parkway and
26th Street
Philadelphia
PA 19130
www.philamuseum.org

San Diego Museum of Art
PO Box 122107
San Diego, California
CA 92112-2107
www.sandiegomuseum.org

Solomon R. Guggenheim Museum
1071 5th Avenue (at 89th Street)
New York
www.guggenheimcollection.org

REST OF THE WORLD

The Israel Museum
POB 71117
Jerusalem 91710
Israel
www.imj.org.il

The State Russian Museum
Mikhailovsky Palace
Inzhenernaya Ulitsa 4
St Petersburg
Russia
www.rusmuseum.ru/eng

Tel Aviv Museum of Art
27 Shaul Hamelech Boulevard
Tel Aviv 64329
Israel
www.tamuseum.com

Index